Table of Contents

Introduction to Judicial Creativity

Unit 4C, concepts of law, is *synoptic*. This means it connects to your other areas of study, not just the substantive law, but the institutions and procedures. You will be expected to show your understanding of these by relating them to the various concepts of law. In this booklet, we cover 'Judicial Creativity'. You should also be able to relate this concept to more contemporary issues and you will find plenty of examples here.

The theory of law is called *jurisprudence*, and is a compulsory part of most law degrees. Many academics, philosophers and judges have written about the theory of law and justice, and there is much disagreement between them.

Examination tip

You are not expected to 'take sides' when discussing the various arguments. You may wish to state your own opinion but if so, be sure to back this up with reference to the theorists and to relevant cases. The main thing when it comes to the examination is to have a clear focus and keep your answer centred on the specific question asked, i.e., keep your answer and examples relevant and, where possible, use one or two of the theorists to support what you say.

Many cases involve several different concepts so you will see cases repeated in the other 'Law Explained' booklets on concepts. Other than cases from the substantive law, e.g., crime, tort or contract, there are numerous contemporary issues which will involve these concepts of law, such as whether it is right to force-feed an anorexic, whether separating Siamese twins knowing one will die is morally justified, whether gays should have equal marriage rights to heterosexuals and many others. All these examples involve questions of morality and justice, but often there are also conflicting interests to be satisfied and occasions where judges have been creative.

Examination tip

It is useful to learn and fully understand cases that can be used across the Unit well, because you can use the same one in different questions – as long as you change the focus. For the higher mark bands, you should develop your points by reference to theorists on the area and/or by arguing for or against the decision.

Example

Taking the case of **Brown**, we can look at how that case can be used to discuss each of the five concepts in Unit 4C AQA Law. This is a very brief outline, as you have not covered all these concepts. However, it should give you an idea of how you can use a case and then adapt and develop it to different situations – a bit like judges do with law.

Concept	Aspect of the case that relates to this concept	Mention of a theorist where possible
Law and Morals	Whether sexual violence in private should be regulated by law rather than purely a matter of morality	**Devlin** would say 'yes' because immoral acts undermine the fabric of society, even when done in private **Hart** would say 'no' because law and morals should be kept separate **Mill** might say 'yes' because he believed in non-interference in individual rights, but could say 'no' because he added 'unless doing so could harm others'
Law and Justice	Whether justice is achieved by imposing legal sanctions against certain behaviour even if it occurs in private	The above could be used again but also a **Utilitarian** would want to see the greatest benefit for the greatest number so could argue that this is achieved by banning the behaviour of the minority to protect society as a whole
Judicial Creativity	Earlier cases conflicted on whether consent was a defence to serious injuries, the majority indicated the ratio was that it was not	Where a *ratio* is unclear, later judges can select the most appropriate or can distinguish the case on the facts. **Professor Goodhard** said, *"It is by his choice of material facts that the judge creates law"* Arguably with such a serious crime Parliament rather than unelected judges should create the law
Fault	It was unclear whether the decision was based on the amount of harm or whether the harm was intentional	*Mens rea* is an important element of criminal law and where harm is committed with intent it should be penalised The acts had been consented to, so it is wrong that the law penalised the behaviour. Even though there was MR the consent defence should have succeeded
Balancing Conflicting Interests	The interests of the public to be protected from violence had to be balanced against the interests of the individuals to act as they pleased in private	**Devlin** would say that society had to be protected from evil, as did some of the judges in **Brown**. **Lord Lowry** said sadomasochism was *"not conducive to the welfare of society"*, and so a **Utilitarian** might agree with the decision. **Pound** believed that public and private interests should not be balanced against each other as the public interest will always prevail, as seen here

The tasks are intended to reinforce your learning so do these as you go along. The answers are at the end of the book. Some tasks will just ask you to jot down a few thoughts for use in an essay, so there are no answers to these, but keep your notes for revision and exam practice. I have included occasional quotes so use these too; they show that you know what judges have to say about the law.

A brief reminder: Criminal cases are usually in the form *R v the defendant*. It is acceptable to use just the name so if the case is **R v Miller** I have called it **Miller**. If another form is used, e.g., **DPP v Miller** I have used the full title, as you may want to look up the case. Civil cases are between the *claimant* ('*plaintiff*' in cases before 1999) and the *defendant*.

There is a list of some common abbreviations in the appendix at the end of the booklet.

Task 1

Before reading on, make a note of the main rules of precedent, then go to the section *Creativity and the rules of precedent'* to check if you included all the rules and to see how they affect creativity. This will also prepare you for Task 2.

"A live system of law will always have regard to changing circumstances"

Lord Keith

When reading this Chapter, keep the following issues in mind. There are several questions to consider, and answers, even in respected academic circles, will differ.

Do judges make law?

How do judges make law?

Should judges make law?

What is the balance between the roles of Parliament and the courts in making law?

Do judges make law?

Whether developing case law or interpreting statutes, judges have a certain amount of discretion. Arguably, this is 'making' law, but opinions differ.

You should have met Professor Hart before in Law and Morals and Law and Justice. Hart would accept that judges make new law and that this is necessary where there are no existing rules to cover the situation, i.e., there are gaps in the law. Another academic, with whom Hart had much debate, is Dworkin. He says judges don't make law but *find* it by using existing legal principles and applying these to new situations.

Example

Hart could see **Donoghue v Stevenson** as *making* a new law (that a manufacturer is liable to the consumer for defective products), which filled in a gap in the existing law. Dworkin could see it as *finding* an existing principle (that people should not harm others), and extending this to a new situation. There is a fine line and no right answer.

Not only academics, but also judges themselves, differ on the issue. Here are a few quotes which could be used in an essay.

A few opinions

In the **Times Law Awards** ceremony 1997, Lord Mackay (the then Lord Chancellor) said, "*The duty of the judge is to apply the law as he finds it, not to seek to rectify perceived inadequacies by the use of creative interpretation*". He also said where there is a gap in the law judges are required to take account of precedent but "*where this is unclear he must decide the best way to proceed and the result may be a decision which is in some way innovative ... but the fundamental principles were always part of the law*". Thus, he believes (along with Dworkin) that judges find law by applying already existing principles.

Similarly, Lord Diplock in **Dupont v Steel 1980** said, "*Parliament makes the laws, the judiciary interpret them*".

Lord Denning would side with Hart, in **Re Sigsworth** he said, "*... we fill in the gaps*".

Austin (a pupil of Jeremy Bentham) was also in favour of judicial law making. He said, "*I cannot understand how any person can suppose ... that society could have gone on if judges had not legislated*".

Examination tip

So, opinions differ on whether judges 'make' or 'find' law. You can offer your own, as long as you support it with cases and examples. Look carefully at the question before you start your answer.

You could be asked whether judges *do* make law, and/or whether they *should* make law. Opinions differ on this latter question too. We'll look at this after seeing *how* they may be creative. Reading case reports is a good idea, as you will see how the judges discussed these issues.

How do judges make law?

Both the rules of precedent and the rules on statutory interpretation involve a certain amount of discretion. The greater the discretion, the more the opportunity for judges to make law.

Some cases involve both precedent and statutory interpretation, so most of the examples come after a brief review of the two sets of rules.

Creativity and the rules of precedent

Although the strict rule of precedent is *stare decisis*, or 'follow what went before' and treat like cases alike, there are many ways to avoid it which allow for creativity. Overruling earlier cases by a higher court or use of the **1966 Practice Statement** by the HL or SC are obvious examples. The **Practice Statement** allowed the HL to overrule its own earlier decisions if '*it appears right to do so*'. This gives a wide discretion and allows an old law to be changed and a new one created.

Example

In **Gemmell & Richards** the HL used the Practice Statement to overrule its earlier decision in **Caldwell**. This changed the old law on objective recklessness and created a new law making all recklessness subjective.

In **Edwards v Environment Agency 2011**, the SC confirmed that it had all the powers previously invested in the HL. So the powers given under the **1966 Practice Statement** have passed to the SC. The **Young** rules allow the CA to overrule its own earlier decisions in certain circumstances, but these are limited so allow little real creativity. Lord Denning wanted the use of the **Practice Statement** to extend to the CA, but he was criticised by many other judges for this view.

Distinguishing can also be creative. A case may be distinguished where material facts are different, and which facts are material may depend on the judge's view. Professor Goodhard said, "*It is by his choice of material facts that the judge creates law*". Finally, the *ratio decidendi* can be difficult to find, especially if the judgment is complex or the reasoning obscure. In the appellate courts, decisions are based on the majority view, so there are several judgments and the reasons for the decision may differ. Judges may agree what the decision *is* but not *why*, thus producing conflicting *ratios*. This allows the later judge to choose which to follow.

Examples

When deciding what the *ratio decidendi* of an earlier case is, a judge may view it broadly and so apply it to new situations, which is 'finding' law in Dworkin's view. Alternatively a judge may take a narrow view and thereby justify distinguishing the *ratio*, which is also somewhat creative. An example is **Donoghue v Stevenson**. A broad view of the *ratio* would be the neighbour principle: we all owe a duty to anyone affected by our acts. A narrow view would be that a manufacturer owes a duty to a consumer. If the narrow view was taken, a later case not involving a manufacture could be distinguished.

In **Brown**, the *ratio* was not clear as there were several complex judgments. It can be argued that the *ratio* was either that a person cannot consent to **serious harm** or that a person cannot consent to **intentional** harm. In **Dica 2004**, the CA followed the latter interpretation of the *ratio* and held that that consent was not a defence to **intentional** harm.

Examination tip

For precedent you need to be clear which rules apply to which courts as this affects how much creativity is possible.

Task 2

Draw a table containing the following rules of precedent and, in the second column, add how far these allow or restrict creativity. Then, in the third column, add a case to illustrate how this works in practice and/or comments to develop the creativity point. The first is done for you as an example.

Stare decisis and original precedent	This doesn't seem to offer much scope for creativity, because judges must follow earlier decisions of all courts above and usually their own. However, higher courts can be creative as they can overrule lower courts, and the Supreme Court (previously the House of Lords) has the greatest scope for creativity as it can overrule any other court and even itself by using the 1966 Practice Statement). Once overruled the old law no longer exists and an original (new) precedent is set.	Creativity can arise if there is no precedent to follow, as in Donoghue v Stephenson where the HL ruled that a manufacturer owed a consumer a duty of care, previously only possible in contract law. This was particularly creative because 1932 was well before the Practice Statement was issued. In R v R 1991, the HL set a precedent that rape within marriage was unlawful, where previously it was not an offence. Lord Keith said "A live system of law will always have regard to changing circumstances."
Ratio decidendi and *obiter dicta*		
Overruling by a higher court or by use of the 1966 Practice Statement		
Distinguishing		

Creativity and statutory interpretation

The **literal rule** means the words of an Act are followed strictly, so cases where this is used can support an argument that judges are *not* creative.

Example

In **Fisher v Bell (1961)**, a shopkeeper who displayed a flick-knife in the window was found not guilty of offering it for sale. Although it was an offence under the **Restriction of Offensive Weapons Act** to 'offer for sale' such weapons, the literal rule was used. The words 'offer for sale' were interpreted strictly under contract law, and in contractual terms, goods in a shop window display are an invitation to treat, not an offer.

The **golden rule** only applies if the **literal rule** leads to absurdity, so allows little creativity. It is not often used, although arguably it should have been used in **Fisher v Bell** because it was absurd that the Act was found not to apply to a situation which it was apparently intended to cover.

Example

In **Allen 1872**, D was charged with bigamy. The wording in the statute said the offence was committed if a married person 'shall marry' another. As marrying for a second time would be void in civil law, using the literal rule would mean the offence could never be committed. The court therefore applied the golden rule to avoid this absurdity and held that the word 'marry' should be interpreted as 'to go through a marriage ceremony'. He was therefore guilty as he had gone through a marriage ceremony for a second time.

The **mischief rule** looks at the 'mischief', or wrongdoing, that the Act was trying to prevent and interprets the statute to avoid that wrongdoing occurring.

Example

In **Smith v Hughes 1960**, the words in a 'street or public place' were interpreted as including a place seen by the public, so prostitutes soliciting from their windows or balconies were guilty under the statute. The mischief the statute aimed to prevent was people being harassed by public soliciting and this interpretation best avoided that wrongdoing.

This case was followed in a slightly different context in **Eastbourne BC v Stirling 2000**. The mischief rule was used when interpreting the words 'plying for hire in any street' in a statute regulating taxis. Here the 'mischief' to be avoided was offering taxi services in public without a licence to do this. The CA held that a driver is plying for hire in the street if his vehicle is positioned so that it is in public view from the street, very much like the prostitutes in **Smith v Hughes**.

The **purposive approach** (developing the **mischief rule**) is more creative. This seeks to give effect to the purpose of legislation by looking at the intention of Parliament and the purpose for which it passed the Act in the first place. Again, **Fisher v Bell** could have benefited from this approach. Although this approach appears to uphold parliamentary sovereignty and the 'finding' law view, it is arguable that judges are putting their own values on what they think Parliament intended. This is particularly true when interpreting an old Act. How can a judge know what Members of Parliament were thinking, e.g., when the **Offences against the Person Act 1861** was passed? The purposive approach, favoured by Lord Denning and more modernist judges, is an extension of the mischief rule, and can mitigate the harshness of the literal rule. In **Pepper v Hart**, Lord Griffiths said, "... *the days have long passed when the courts adopted a strict constructionist view of interpretation*". He favoured the purposive approach, but in order to use the purposive approach it is, of course, necessary to try to find out what Parliament's intention was at the time the Act was passed. This requires use of external aids such as Hansard and Law Commission reports. **Pepper** was itself creative because it allowed the use of Hansard (containing the debates in Parliament during the passing of the Act) for the first time.

Example

The purposive approach was seen in **Clinton 2012**, where the CA used Hansard to look at the parliamentary debates during the passing of the **Coroners and Justice Act**, when interpreting a section of it. The purpose of the Act as a whole was also considered when determining that sexual infidelity could be included in **s 54(1)** in regard to what characteristics could be taken into account.

Examination tip

When giving case examples of how interpretation works you need to be clear about what the judge is doing. This means highlighting the words in the Act that are being interpreted and showing how the way they were interpreted affected the result. The following task will help with this. You can then refer back to these examples when assessing how far judges should be developing the law, with a brief comment on whether you think the result achieved what Parliament intended.

Example

The mischief rule was used in **Smith v Hughes 1960**, where the statute prohibited prostitutes soliciting 'in a street or public place'. The judge decided Parliament intended to prevent soliciting in a public place, so interpreted the words to include places seen by the public. Prostitutes were found guilty of soliciting from windows and balconies because they could be seen from the street.

See Task 3 for more examples.

Task 3

Draw a table showing the different approaches to interpretation, with a case on each. Include a brief reference to the words or Act being interpreted, as in the example of the literal rule. Keep this and your table from the previous task as a base on which to build some ideas about how far judges are being creative – or not. Refer to these as you read this Chapter and where possible add a few more cases to them which you can use in an essay.

The literal rule	Taking the words of a statute literally means judges are not being creative.	Fisher v Bell – interpreting the words 'offer for sale' to include goods in a shop window.
The golden rule		
The mischief rule		
The purposive approach		

Judges must consider the **Human Rights Act** when interpreting statutes and this could lead to a more creative judgment where the law infringes rights protected by the **European Convention on Human Rights (ECHR)**, as in **Campbell v MGN 2004**. See under 'other matters' for more on this.

Task 4

Before going on, make a note of three cases where you feel the judges have been creative (or not) in using the rules outlined above.

Here are a few examples from each area of substantive law; crime, contract and tort. There are plenty of others you could use instead.

Examination tip

As you need to evaluate and analyse the law at this level it is a good idea to use cases you are comfortable with. I have tried to include several illustrations from each area, but don't use my examples if you don't fully understand them. Choose your own. This will mean you are more confident in explaining how creative the decision was and which rules allowed or restricted this. It is difficult to evaluate or analyse a case if you do not appreciate exactly what it involved.

Crime

Brown on sado-masochism is arguably creative. The question was whether consensual injuries could amount to a crime under the **Offences against the Person Act** or common law. The **Act** did not deal with consent, and at common law, cases conflicted on whether it was a defence to serious injuries.

This decision distinguishes earlier cases based on the amount of harm that occurred. However, even the judges themselves were unclear on the reason for their decisions. The case was decided on a 3-2 majority. Lord Slynn thought the precedents cited were not conclusive and said it is *"a matter of policy for the legislature to decide"*. Lord Mustill also thought it was a matter for Parliament. He said if the level of harm amounted to assault regardless of consent then deciding whether private sexual activities should be exempt was *"a task which the courts are not suited to perform"*. The other three judges thought the courts *should* intervene to protect society as a whole; Lord Templeman saying that pleasure derived from pain was evil.

In **R v R**, the HL interpreted the **Sexual Offences Act 1956** in a creative way, and held that a man could be guilty of raping his wife. Until this case, it was not rape as a wife was deemed to consent to sexual intercourse by marrying. Lord Keith said that the common law was *"capable of evolving in the light of changing social, economic and cultural developments"*.

In **Gemmell & Richards**, the HL used the **Practice Statement** to overrule the decision in **Caldwell** and create a new rule that all recklessness is now subjective.

Camplin overruled **Bedder** when interpreting the **Homicide Act** and set a precedent. **Smith** was even more creative but shows judges were divided, and in **Holley**, the Privy Council rejected **Smith** and said D was to be judged against a person having *"ordinary powers of self-control"*. Although Privy Council decisions are not *strictly binding*, they are made by Law Lords so this decision was highly *persuasive*. The desire for Parliament to act was apparent in the judgments, which showed a reluctance for further judicial development. The **Coroners and Justice Act 2009** has now put **Holley** into statutory form in the new defence of loss of control, which refers to a person with *"a normal degree of tolerance and self-restraint"*. Also, in **Clinton 2012**, the CA interpreted the **Act** as excluding sexual infidelity if it was the only trigger relied on, but allowing it to be taken into account as one of the circumstances of D under **s 54(1)**. To do this they referred to various speeches in Parliament during the passing of the Act and also looked at the Act as a whole, a purposive approach to the legislation.

Task 5

> *What type of precedent was set in Holley?*
> *What effect does this type of precedent have?*
> *Why might it be followed?*
> *What effect did the Coroners and Justice Act have?*

Contract

There is perhaps less creativity in contract, as judges are reluctant to intervene in the rights of people to be free to make their own contracts. This is one of the reasons there are so many old cases in contract; they have remained undisturbed over the years. However, there are still many examples to be found.

Taylor v Caldwell set a precedent in establishing the doctrine of frustration.

Adams v Linsell established the postal rule (though many argue it is time that judges got creative again and abolished it!).

In **Pereira (J) Fernandes SA v Metha 2006**, the court held that an e-mail is sufficient to support an agreement which is required to be in writing. This is an example of judges reacting to new technology, as the previous law had only dealt with other types of written agreements and not electronic ones. However, the argument that the e-mail address itself amounted to a signature was rejected; this would be too creative. The court held that a signature had to be more than incidental and must clearly relate to the whole document.

Merritt distinguished **Balfour** on the presumption that in social arrangements the parties do not intend to be legally bound.

Williams v Roffey distinguished earlier cases such as **Stilk** so that consideration could be 'found' even though there was little evidence of it.

The Moorcock introduced the idea that courts could intervene in order to give 'business efficacy' to contracts.

Fisher v Bell could be used to show how *lack* of creativity on the part of judges can lead to an Act being ineffective. Use of the purposive approach, or even the golden 'rule', could have resulted in a conviction.

In **Dunnachie v Hull CC 2004,** the HL followed **Addis v Gramophone Co Ltd** and refused to allow damages for non-pecuniary loss, such as hurt feelings or loss of enjoyment, in unfair dismissal cases. Creativity in this area is restricted to 'holiday' cases where enjoyment is an important part of what was contracted for.

Tort

As discussed earlier, **Donoghue** set a precedent but it could be argued either way as to whether this was 'filling a gap in the law' (as viewed by Hart or Lord Denning) or 'applying existing principles' of not harming others to a new situation (as viewed by Dworkin and Lord Mackay).

In **McLoughlin v O'Brien**, the law on nervous shock was developed by the HL, but in **Alcock**, Lord Oliver indicated that further developments should be left to Parliament.

BRB v Herrington was an early use of the Practice Statement by the HL which overruled the case of **Addie v Dumbreck** and allowed child trespassers to sue an occupier in negligence. This then led to the passing of the **Occupier's Liability Act 1984**, showing that a creative judiciary can also persuade Parliament to create new law.

In **Hunter v Canary Wharf 1997**, the HL applied the existing principle that there was no right of action for blocking a view; to find interference with television reception was not actionable in nuisance. In **Network Rail v Morris 2004**, this was followed in respect to electromagnetic interference caused to a recording studio. It is arguable that in this day and age most people watch TV and the law should be more creative and offer some protection against electronic interference.

Rylands v Fletcher can be seen as filling a gap in the law, but the rule was introduced by analogy with the law on damage by fire and animals, so was arguably only extending existing principles to other 'dangerous' things. In **Cambridge Water**, the judges showed reluctance to develop the law in this area. Lord Goff said, *"... it is more appropriate for strict liability in respect of operations of high risk to be imposed by Parliament than by the courts".* **Transco** also shows such reluctance.

Essay pointer

In **Lister v Halsey Hall**, the HL held employers could be vicariously liable for the sexual acts of an employee. This overruled the decision in **Trotman** that a school was not vicariously liable for a teacher's sexual activities during a school trip. Clearly such acts are not authorised but in **Lister** the HL held his acts were sufficiently connected to his employment (as a warden in a boys' school). There has been much debate about cases like these and some argue **Lister** was too creative. It is a difficult issue because the law needs to protect people, especially the young, but finding an employer liable for something that is hard to regulate seems unfair.

Examination tip

Practice discussing both sides of an argument about how creative a decision is or whether judges should create law. This will help you to write a balanced essay in an examination which will always gain more marks than a one-sided monologue. The following task will help with this, as will tasks 8, 9 and 10.

Task 6

In **Donoghue v Stevenson**, the HL decided that a manufacturer owed a duty to a consumer without the need for a contract between them. Do you think the judges were right to be creative? Give one argument for and one against.

Other matters

In **Nicklinson 2013**, the CA held that it was not appropriate to create a defence of necessity in cases of euthanasia and assisted suicide and that it was *"such a complex and controversial field"* that it was properly a matter for Parliament. The CA also noted that the wording of the **Suicide Act** made it clear that assisted suicide was a serious criminal offence carrying a maximum sentence of 14 years' imprisonment. In those circumstances the court could not, and should not, interpret the Act so as to develop a defence to assisted suicide.

In **Douglas v Hello**!, Hello! magazine published unauthorised photographs of the wedding between Catherine Zeta-Jones and Michael Douglas and they, and OK! magazine, which had been authorised to publish photographs, took Hello! to court. The case ran for many years and the courts were not in agreement. In the High court Lindsay J said that it was *"better left to Parliament"* to develop the law on privacy but ruled that there was a 'breach of confidence'. However, this decision was reversed by the CA. Then in **Douglas v Hello! 2008**, the HL reversed the CA's decision and reinstated the decision of Lindsay J. This was only by a 3-2 majority though, and the judgments were long and complex.

In **Campbell v MGN 2004**, the model Naomi Campbell won a case against MGN for publishing photographs of her leaving a Narcotics Anonymous meeting, with comments that she was a drug addict. The decision was reversed by the CA and but on appeal to the HL it was held that her right to privacy under **Article 8 (ECHR)** outweighed MGN's right to freedom of expression under **Article 10**. This was again only by a 3-2 majority.

In **Murray v Express Newspapers & Others 2008**, the author of the Harry Potter books, J.K. Rowling, won a case brought on behalf of her young son against a photographic agency for publishing secretly taken photographs of him. The CA held that the law should protect children from intrusive media attention but went on to say that this did not mean there was a guarantee of privacy and also that the decision could be different in the case of an adult.

These cases show a limited creativity by judges in the absence of any action by Parliament. However, the various appeals and reversals show that, as Lindsay J said, it would be better if an elected Parliament were to act.

Another problem is that judge-made law relies on someone bringing a case to court, and carrying the case on through the appeal process to the higher courts. This is not only random, it is time-consuming and expensive. Michael Douglas, Naomi Campbell and J.K.Rowling may well have the funds to ask the law to protect their privacy, but this is not true of most people.

When looking at cases and other examples think about whether judges *should* be creative, and the different roles of Parliament and the courts. Let's look at these two issues.

Should judges make law?

The main argument for judges being creative is that rules are rarely absolute. They cannot provide for all that the future may bring. Hart says because rules are indeterminate, i.e., they have an 'open texture', judges must 'fill in the gaps', a point Lord Denning made several times. If a new situation arises, such as text-messaging scams or internet abuse, a judge has to decide the matter and can hardly say 'the rules have run out so I can't make a judgment'. The judge uses the tools available, the rules on precedent and interpretation, to come to a decision. Again, opinions differ and the idea of 'filling in the gaps' is not approved of by many judges. Lord Diplock, in **Duport Steels Ltd v Sirs 1980**, argued that this approach could only be used if there was ambiguity in the law, i.e., if the literal rule couldn't be used. As we saw, Lord Mackay said that the duty of the judge is *"to apply the law as he finds it, not to seek to rectify perceived inadequacies by the use of creative interpretation"*. In this view it is Parliament who should make the law, and if the law is inadequate then Parliament should amend it. Having said that, it is not always realistic, e.g., judges have to interpret the **Offences against the Person Act** which was passed in 1861 and is full of ambiguous and archaic language, but despite the difficulties and numerous calls for reform, Parliament has not amended it.

Task 7

Before going on can you think of three reasons why a judge may need to be creative?

Not only does technology change, so do social values. E.g., in **R v R**, it was felt no longer acceptable to allow marital immunity against a charge of rape. Lord Keith made the opening comment. However, he agreed with Lord Lane's comment in the CA that, *"This is not the creation of a new offence, it is the removal of a common law fiction which has become anachronistic and offensive"*. An argument against judges being creative is that the law should not be used to enforce morality (reinforcing Hart's point that law and morals should be separate). In **Brown,** some judges seemed to base their decision on what was morally right. Arguably, this is not a good basis for finding criminal behaviour, and it is for Parliament to decide on such matters after a proper debate on the issue.

In **Nicklinson 2013**, the CA held that it was not for judges to create a defence of necessity in cases of euthanasia and assisted suicide but a matter for Parliament. It was acknowledged that where the statute was clear it was not possible to interpret it in such a way as to develop the law.

Essay pointer

Consider whether society should lead and the law follow or the other way round? E.g., in relation to homosexuality and prostitution, as society changed and became more tolerant, the law eventually changed to reflect this. In some cases, this is left to Parliament but enacting law is usually a lengthy process and the courts can develop the common law to meet changing conditions more quickly. New technology leads to new legal problems; case law can respond to such problems as they occur, as in **Quintavalle**.

A strong argument against creativity is that if a judge makes law it applies retrospectively, at least to the parties in court. In **R v R** (and possibly **Brown**) it would be difficult to find a law stating the behaviour was a crime at the time of the acts. That someone can be guilty of a crime which appears not to have existed at the time it was committed is arguably unjust. When Parliament makes a law it only applies to the future, i.e., it is forbidden to do this *from now on*. This brings us to the differing roles of Parliament and the courts.

The balance between the roles of Parliament and the courts

Parliament is elected. Members of Parliament are our representatives and so can be said to make laws on our behalf, to protect society as a whole. Most people accept Parliament's *right* to make law, even if not agreeing with a particular law. Judges are not elected so people may find it harder to accept their role in law making, especially if this involves a matter of policy. In **McLoughlin v O'Brien**, Lord Scarman said, *"the objective of judges is the formulation of principles, policy is the prerogative of Parliament"*. He felt any creativity had to be based on legal principle and not policy. Policy is concerned with what is right for society as a whole, a collective goal. The government formulates a policy, e.g., to ban smoking in public, produces a Bill aimed at fulfilling that policy, and puts it before Parliament for debating and voting on. Many think policy should *only* be a matter for government and Parliament. However, judges are clearly involved in policy decisions and often take the wider community interests into account.

Examples

In **Hill v CC of West Yorkshire** the 'fair, just and reasonable' requirement in relation to proving a duty of care was used to find the police did not owe a duty as it was not in the public interest. In **Miller v Jackson**, the wider community benefit of cricket outweighed her interests, so that an injunction to stop it was refused.

The main point in favour of creativity is the ability of the courts to react to situations as they arise. **Quintavalle** is an example of the judiciary reacting to a situation that needed an immediate answer (whether a couple could use tissue typing to choose an embryo for IVF treatment). Other examples are the developments in relation to privacy.

Essay pointer

There are sound arguments on both sides of the 'should judges make law?' question. The need for certainty and consistency suggests always following the letter of the law, using the strict rule of precedent and the literal rule where possible. However, justice in a particular case may indicate a need to be creative, as will changing technology and social values. One problem is that in precedent the later judge finds the *ratio* and decides which facts are material, and in statutory interpretation, the judge chooses which rule to use. This means different judges may come to different decisions on the same set of facts, leading to inconsistency.

The fact that judges are not elected and Parliament is supreme supports the view that judges should not make law. This may be why judges often try to give the appearance of 'finding' law, even when it can be said that they are 'making' it. Some explicitly recognise it is not their job, as we saw by Lord Goff's comment in **Cambridge Water**.

A final point which can support judicial creativity is precisely that Parliament *is* supreme, so any decision of any court can be reversed. In **Axa General Insurance v the Lord Advocate 2011**, hailed as a 'landmark judgment', the Supreme Court held that the Scottish Parliament was within its rights to pass a new law restoring pleural plaques victims' right to compensation. The new law effectively reverses the controversial decision of the HL in **Rothwell v Chemical & Insulating Co 2007**, which rejected claims for compensation because the plaques themselves had had no effect, and there was no action in tort in respect of a risk of future injury. The UK Parliament has yet to act on this, but an example of statute law reversing a creative decision by the judiciary is when Parliament added an amendment to the **Compensation Act 2006** to reverse the decision in **Barker v Corus 2006** (where the HL held that if there was more than one cause of harm, damages could be apportioned according to how far each D had materially increased the risk of injury). If a judge gets too innovative, Parliament can step in, so there is a limit on any such creativity.

In some cases, Parliament will show its agreement with a decision by passing a law putting it into statutory form, as happened with the **Human Fertilisation and Embryology Act 1990 2008** following the **Quintavalle** decision. The **Occupiers' Liability Act 1984** is another example of this, following **BRB v Herringto**n. This seems a good balance because if there are moral or otherwise controversial issues at stake then there can be a full consultation with the public followed by debates in Parliament before a law is passed. Perhaps this is a good compromise; the courts can react to the immediate situation and Parliament can then debate the matter. If Parliament does not agree with the decision then it can enact a new law to reverse it as with the **Compensation Act**.

Task 8

Read through the chapter noting down a few of the different opinions on whether judges make law. Write a paragraph or two with arguments for and/or against creativity and develop these using some of the quotes and cases to illustrate. This will help you to produce your own arguments which can be used for an essay on the subject.

Self-test questions

Why might a judge need to be creative?

Give two arguments against judicial creativity.

Why does Hart say judges must 'fill in the gaps'?

Who else said this?

Who argues that judges are merely applying existing principle and not making law?

A general guide to revision

The first and foremost rule for revision is to start early. Too many students leave it until the last minute and then get in a panic. If you take it gently and organise your time properly you will feel a lot more calm and confident when exam time comes. Make a plan of what you want to cover each day and try to stick to it. Don't forget to include some breaks in your schedule, if you are tired it will be harder to retain the material you have been revising.

Here are a few tips for revision techniques

> *Go through your notes and try to summarise them*
>
> *Learn the key cases, as these are essential to know*
>
> *Make sure you understand how the judge has applied the law to the facts so you can do the same in an examination scenario*
>
> *If the case is one you may also want to use in an essay, be sure you understand any problems it raises or solves and/or the concept of law that is involved*

Example

In **Brown**, the judges decided that consent was not a defence to serious harm, so this would apply to a scenario involving GBH.

It raises a problem in the law, because the reasoning was obscure. It was not sufficiently clear why the consent defence failed. It could be argued that the defence fails if harm was intended (this would apply to **s 18** but not **s 20**), or alternatively that the defence fails if harm was serious (this would apply to both **s 18** and **s 20**).

Another problem, and one which relates to the concept of creativity, is that some judges seemed to rely on their own moral values when reaching their decision. It is arguable that Parliament should make such decisions, not judges, because Parliament not only debates the issue but also usually precedes legislation with a public consultation. A particular problem with the **Offences against the Person Act** is that it difficult for judges to know what Parliament's intention or purpose was, because it is such an old Act with ambiguous and obscure language.

> *Go through the summaries of the topic, these provide a base of the essential points which may need to be addressed*
>
> *Go to the examination board's website for past exam papers, mark schemes and reports*
>
> *Practice answering questions then look at the examiners' mark schemes and reports to see if you were on the right track*

Revision of creativity

A brief reminder of the effect of precedent on creativity

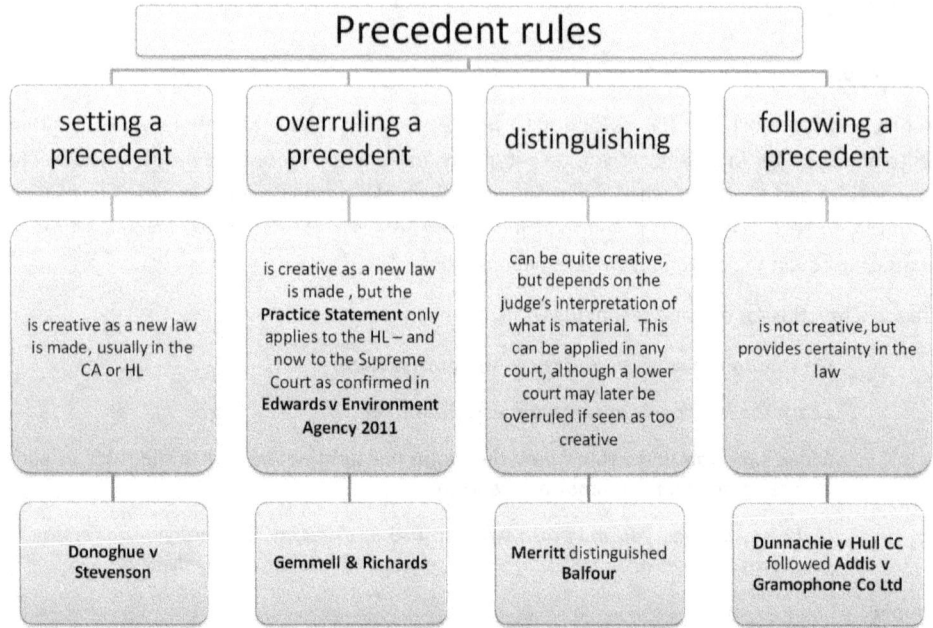

Precedent rules

setting a precedent	overruling a precedent	distinguishing	following a precedent
is creative as a new law is made, usually in the CA or HL	is creative as a new law is made, but the **Practice Statement** only applies to the HL – and now to the Supreme Court as confirmed in **Edwards v Environment Agency 2011**	can be quite creative, but depends on the judge's interpretation of what is material. This can be applied in any court, although a lower court may later be overruled if seen as too creative	is not creative, but provides certainty in the law
Donoghue v Stevenson	**Gemmell & Richards**	**Merritt** distinguished **Balfour**	**Dunnachie v Hull CC** followed **Addis v Gramophone Co Ltd**

Task 9

Note down one argument for and against distinguishing

A brief reminder of the effect of statutory interpretation on creativity

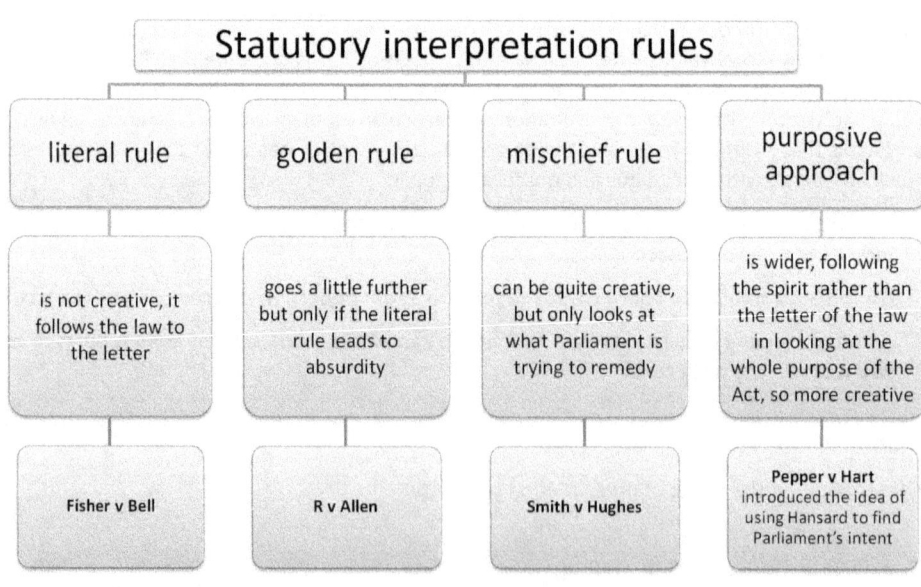

Statutory interpretation rules

literal rule	golden rule	mischief rule	purposive approach
is not creative, it follows the law to the letter	goes a little further but only if the literal rule leads to absurdity	can be quite creative, but only looks at what Parliament is trying to remedy	is wider, following the spirit rather than the letter of the law in looking at the whole purpose of the Act, so more creative
Fisher v Bell	**R v Allen**	**Smith v Hughes**	**Pepper v Hart** introduced the idea of using Hansard to find Parliament's intent

Should judges make law? Balance the roles of the courts and Parliament.

Parliament is seen as the supreme law maker as it is democratically elected. Judges may have to be creative at times to 'fill in the gaps' but Parliament will often then follow the decision with new legislation to put it in statutory form. If a judge were to be too creative Parliament can pass a new Act to change the law created.

Examples

Donoghue v Stevenson was eventually followed by the **Consumer Protection Act 1967** which strengthened the law protecting consumers as created in **Donoghue**

BRB v Herrington was followed by the **Occupiers' Liability Act 1984** which added to the 1957 Act to put the creative decision protecting 'non-visitors' into statutory form

R v R was followed by amendments to the **Sexual Offences Act** to bring the Act into line with the House of Lords ruling

Quintavalle was followed by the **Human Fertilisation and Embryology Act 1990 2008** to allow tissue typing to be licensed where a sibling suffers from a serious medical condition

Barker v Corus 2006 was *not* followed by Parliament when it passed the **Compensation Act 2006** to reverse the creative ruling on apportioning damages

Task 10

Discussing both sides of an argument will help you to write a balanced essay in an examination. Using the following case to illustrate, briefly argue both for and against judges making law. If possible add a reference to one of the theorists.

In **R v R** the HL decided that there was no longer immunity for a husband who raped his wife

Opinions differ not only on whether judges do make law but also on whether they should. Read back through some of the opinions before going on (and then see Task 11).

Examination tip

You can answer a question on creativity by reference to precedent or statutory interpretation, or both. Read the question carefully to make sure you are not being directed to one or the other, though. Also note that at this level you need to discuss both the rules and the ways to avoid them, using cases and opinions to relate your discussion to the specific question.

A general guide to examination papers

Read **all** questions carefully before deciding which to answer.

Look again at the ones you wish to answer to make sure you can do so, make brief notes – this can be a useful checklist later when you are tired and your memory begins to fail.

Structure your answer. A solid start is worth a lot and gets the examiner on your side. A small plan is helpful.

It is necessary to do more than regurgitate your notes. Never put in irrelevant material just because you know it – there is **never** a question asking you to 'write all you know about...'. You need to be selective as to what is relevant, and choose appropriate cases and examples in support of what you say.

In essay questions, you will usually be asked to form an opinion or to weigh up arguments for and against a particular statement. Here a broader range of knowledge is needed showing arguments for, arguments against and an evaluation of these arguments. You should always round off your answer with a short concluding paragraph, preferably using some of the wording from the question to indicate to the examiner that you are addressing the specific issue raised.

Essays should have a logical structure. The beginning should introduce the subject matter, the central part should explain/analyse/criticise it as appropriate, and the conclusion should bring the various strands of argument together with reference to the question set.

Try to consider alternative arguments. A well-rounded essay will bring in other views even if you disagree with them; you cannot shoot them down without setting them up first.

Essay writing is a skill in itself, so here is a brief guide on how to structure your essay.

Writing a discussion essay: staging the information logically

If you stage your essay as follows, it will make it easy to read, logically structured and easier to write. It may also mean you don't leave out important points. Here's how it works:

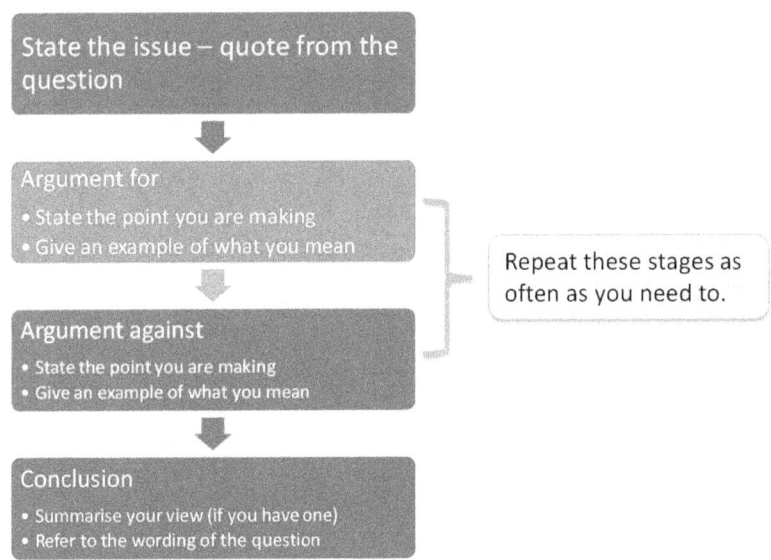

Writing each paragraph: making each one logical and easy to read (and write!)

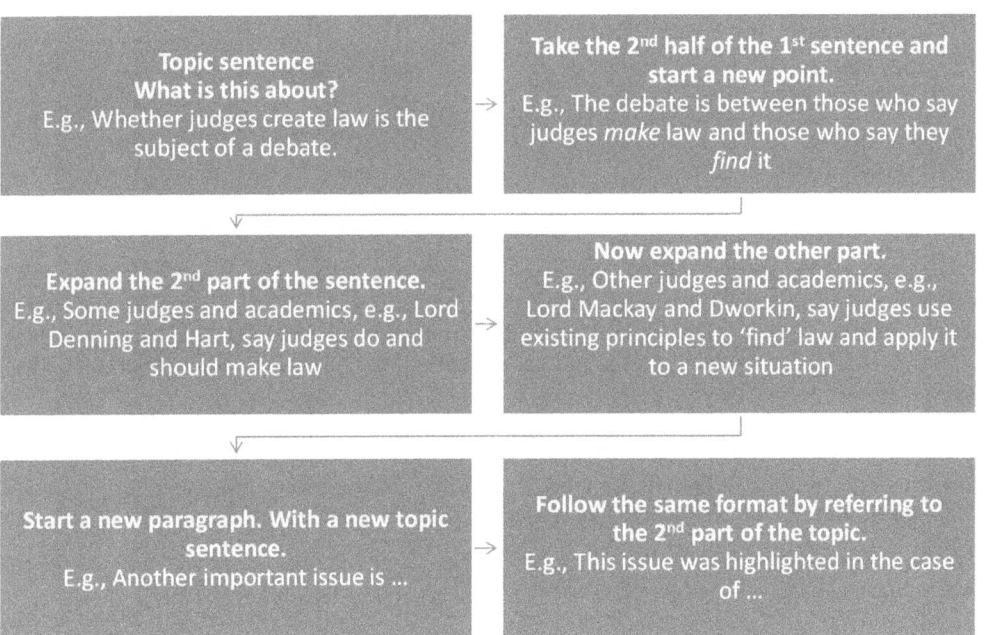

Finally, make sure you cover the whole question; there are only a certain number of marks available. The examiner has a mark scheme to work to, so however brilliant your answer to one part of the question is, missing out the other parts will severely reduce your total marks.

Examination practice for judicial creativity

Although different exam boards have different ways of styling their examination papers, there are always going to be common elements. You will need to be able to evaluate a given concept to provide a critique of the area, including case examples and reference to judicial and academic opinions where appropriate.

The 'Essay pointers' and 'Tasks' provide you with information to use in an essay. Look through these before doing the examination practice tasks below.

There are no 'Key criticisms' in this booklet because there is no particular law to criticise; there are only different views on how far judges make law, and how far they should do so.

Examination tip

Don't forget that you need to be clear about what the judge is doing; we saw that with precedent you need to explain which rules apply to which courts. You also need to state which rules the judge used to come to the particular decision in your case examples. For statutory interpretation you need to refer to the words in the Act that are being interpreted and explain how the rule used affected the result.

Task 11 Examination practice

Many examination questions ask you to consider not only how judges make law, but also whether they should. Write a sentence or two giving the views of the following people on whether judges should make law.

   Lord Denning

   Lord Mackay

   Professor Hart

   Lord Diplock

   Lord Keith

Examination tip

As with most of the concepts of law questions, there may be similarities in the questions, but look carefully to make sure you get the emphasis right. You can prepare a basic answer to this type of question but you will need to be able to adapt it to cover the specific point raised. Look carefully at the wording and make sure you answer the actual question, not the one you hoped to get which you saw in an earlier paper.

Task 12 Examination practice

Write an essay (around 400 words) on whether you think judges should make law. Include some reference to academic or judicial opinions or debates surrounding the particular area.

Remember, although there is no 'right' answer to evaluation questions and opinions vary, if you offer your own opinion **always** use cases and/or examples to back up what you say.

Examination question: Task 13

The following is an example of a typical examination question.

'Discuss to what extent judges can develop the law through the use of precedent and statutory interpretation and consider whether they should do so'

Using the following as a guide, write out a detailed plan of what you would include in an answer to this question.

A logical approach is needed so that you keep on track of the actual question, and do not wander into irrelevant areas. It is best to divide a question like this into several parts.

A brief plan would look something like this:

An explanation of the rules of precedent and statutory interpretation

A discussion of whether judges make law, with examples and reference to the above

An evaluation of the extent to which judges make law, with examples and reference to judicial and academic opinions

An evaluation of the extent to which judges should make law, with examples and reference to judicial and academic opinions

Answers to self-test questions and tasks

Task 1

The answer is by reference to the section 'Creativity and the rules of precedent' which followed the task

Task 2

Here is a guide but there are many other examples you can use. It is always best to choose ones that make sense to you as this will help you to explain them well.

Stare decisis and original precedent	This doesn't seem to offer much scope for creativity, because judges must follow earlier decisions of all courts above and usually their own. However, higher courts can be creative as they can overrule lower courts, and the Supreme Court (previously the House of Lords) has the greatest scope for creativity as it can overrule any other court and even itself by using the 1966 Practice Statement). Once overruled the old law no longer exists and an original (new) precedent is set.	Creativity can arise if there is no precedent to follow, as in Donoghue v Stephenson where the HL ruled that a manufacturer owed a consumer a duty of care, previously only possible in contract law. This was particularly creative because 1932 was well before the Practice Statement was issued. In R v R 1991, the HL set a precedent that rape within marriage was unlawful, where previously it was not an offence. Lord Keith said "A live system of law will always have regard to changing circumstances."
Ratio decidendi and obiter dicta	This allows some creativity as it is the later judge who decides what the ratio is. Decisions in appeal courts are based on a majority, so there are several judgments and thus more than one possible ratio. The later judge can 'find' the preferred ratio, allowing a certain amount of creativity. Obiter dicta do not have to be followed but can be persuasive, especially where they appeared in a decision of a higher court.	One possible ratio in **Donoghue** is that a manufacturer owes a consumer a duty of care, but it has been developed and applied to many other situations; some judges viewed the obiter dicta as the ratio (see below). In **Donoghue** obiter dicta in the House of Lords, that one should take care not to harm one's neighbour, were followed in many later cases not involving a manufacturer or consumer.
Overruling by a higher court or by use of the 1966 Practice Statement	This allows for creativity because old laws can be changed and new ones created. The limit on creativity is that the Practice Statement only applies to the Supreme Court, and in the interests of certainty is not often used.	In **Gemmell & Richards 2003**, the House of Lords overruled its decision in **Caldwell** by using the Practice Statement. This abolished objective recklessness and made a new rule that all recklessness is subjective.
Distinguishing	This allows for creativity because an earlier case may be distinguished where the material facts are different, and the later judge can decide what is material. Professor Goodhard, an academic, said "It is by his choice of material facts that the judge creates law."	This is very common as cases very rarely have identical material facts. One example is **Watson**, where the CA distinguished **Dawson** because the man's frailty was clear in the later case

The literal rule	Taking the words of a statute literally means judges are not being creative.	Fisher v Bell – interpreting the words 'offer for sale' to include goods in a shop window.
The golden rule	This only applies if the literal rule leads to absurdity, so also allows very little creativity.	Allen – interpreting the word 'marry' to mean 'to go through a marriage ceremony'.
The mischief rule	This is more creative as judges can consider the policy behind the statute and what harm it was trying to prevent.	Smith v Hughes – interpreting the words 'public place' to include places seen from the street.
The purposive approach	This is the most creative approach in that judges themselves can decide what they think Parliament intended and then attempt to achieve the intended purpose of the statute.	Clinton – interpreting the Coroners and Justice Act 2009 as allowing sexual infidelity as a characteristic even though not as a qualifying trigger.

Task 4

Several examples from crime, contract and tort are given in the text following this task

Task 5

The precedent in **Holley** was a persuasive precedent

The effect of this type of precedent is that it is not binding on future cases

It might be followed because Law Lords sit on the Privy Council and so it is a bit like a judgment of the HL (or SC)

The **Coroners and Justice Act** put **Holley** into statutory form so it is now the law even though originally only a persuasive precedent

Task 6

For: Judges making law means the law can act to do justice, based on the particular facts of the case. In this case the woman was ill through the negligence of the manufacturer. As Mrs Donoghue did not buy the drink she had no action against him in contract, so it was fair for the HL to change the law to protect her, and to protect other consumers following the case.

Against: Judges making law means the law applied retrospectively which seems wrong. An Act of Parliament looks to control future behaviour which is fair because people know (or can find out) what is against the law. In this case the manufacturer may have been negligent but at the time it was not illegal unless there was a contract between the consumer and the manufacturer.

Task 7

Three possible reasons that a judge may need to be creative are:

Changes in moral values as in R v R

Changes in technology or medicine which mean events of the case were not foreseen, as in Quintavalle

Ambiguity or poor wording in a statute as in the Offences against the Person Act 1861

Task 8

There are valid arguments for and against creativity and many different opinions as to whether it happens, and if so whether it should. Here is an argument for and against supported by academic or judicial opinions and illustrated by a couple of familiar cases.

"Judges may need to make law to fill in gaps where there is no precedent or Act to cover the particular circumstances which have arisen, as in **Quintavalle**. Hart recognised that creativity may be necessary where there are no existing rules to cover the situation. Lord Denning would have agreed, in **Re Sigsworth** he said, "… *we fill in the gaps*". Austin was also in favour of judicial law making. He said, "*I cannot understand how any person can suppose … that society could have gone on if judges had not legislated*". The decision in **R v R** would illustrate this as the judges felt society had moved on and no longer saw marital rape as acceptable, thus the law needed to be adjusted to keep up with changing values. Lord Keith said "*A live system of law will always have regard to changing circumstances*". In **Donoghue v Stevenson** a new law was created to give consumers protection against negligent manufacturers. There was a gap in the law because previously only those with a contract had protection, filling the gap provided justice for all consumers.

"Judges should not make law because they are not elected, unlike Parliament. As Lord Diplock said in **Dupont v Steel**, "*Parliament makes the laws, the judiciary interpret them*". Lord Mackay did not think judges should make law. He said, "*The duty of the judge is to apply the law as he finds it, not to seek to rectify perceived inadequacies by the use of creative interpretation*". He would prefer Parliament to make the law, and if that law is inadequate judges should not try to amend it by being creative. He recognised that there may be gaps in the law, but thought judges should rely on existing principles to fill these gaps, rather than making a new law. Dworkin also believed that judges find law by applying existing principles to new situations. In this view, the judges in **Donoghue v Stevenson** filled the gap in the law by using the existing principle that people should not harm others, and extending this to different circumstances. In **R v R** Lord Keith said "*This is not the creation of a new offence*". He preferred to see it as removing something that was out-dated and offensive from the existing common law, but this is a fine line to draw and someone was convicted of what was arguably a new offence created by judges rather than an elected Parliament (although Parliament later legislated to put the decision into statutory form)."

Self-test questions

Judges need to be creative to keep up with social or technological changes

Two arguments against creativity would be that judges are not elected and that when a government produces a bill which then goes through Parliament there is time for debates and consultations

Hart say judges must 'fill in the gaps' because laws have an open-ended nature and are not complete

Lord Denning also said this

Dworkin argues that judges are merely applying existing principles and not making law

An argument for distinguishing is that it allows for some discretion on the part of the judge. This means an earlier decision need not be followed even if made by a higher court. An example is **Watson** where **Dawson** was distinguished. This was right because the burglars knew the man was frail but carried on with their burglary. If **Dawson** had been followed they would not have been guilty of manslaughter.

The problem with distinguishing is that it can mean the law is unpredictable. The basic rule of precedent is *stare decisis* and this helps keep the law consistent. Distinguishing where material facts are different seems acceptable, but different judges may have different ideas of what is material. Professor Goodhard said, "*It is by his choice of material facts that the judge creates law*". Discretion may sometimes be necessary but too much discretion means uncertainty.

For: Judges making law means the law can adapt to social changes or provide practical solutions to real-life situations. In this case society no longer deemed it appropriate for a woman to be treated as belonging to her husband so that she had no right to refuse sexual relations. The HL was right to make this decision because Parliament had not changed the law which was out-dated and unjust. As Devlin has said, society needs protecting from immoral behaviour.

Against: Judges making law means the law applied retrospectively. An Act of Parliament looks to control future behaviour which is fair because people know what is against the law. In this case the man may have been wrong to act as he did but at the time it was not illegal. The fact that it was immoral should not have led to the judge making such a decision. As Hart pointed out, law and morals should be separate.

Lord Denning thought judges *should* make law. He said 'we fill in the gaps' and also wanted the use of the **Practice Statement** to extend to the CA which would allow more creativity.

Lord Mackay thought judges *should not* make law. He thought the duty of judges was to apply the law as it was and not to try to put it right 'by the use of creative interpretation'.

Professor Hart thought judges *should* make law. He said that because rules are indeterminate, i.e., they have an 'open texture', judges must 'fill in the gaps'.

Lord Diplock thought judges *should not* make law. He said 'Parliament makes the laws, the judiciary interpret them'.

Lord Keith thought judges *should* make law. He said the law should 'have regard to changing circumstances' and should evolve 'in the light of changing social, economic and cultural developments'.

"In some cases I think judges should make law because it means the law can do justice, based on the particular facts. An example is **Donoghue v Stevenson** where a woman was ill because of the negligence of the manufacturer. At the time the law only protected those with a contract, so it seems fair for the HL to develop the law to protect all consumers. Similarly in **BRB v Herrington** the law was developed to extend protection to 'non-visitors'. Judges also may need to be creative due to changes in moral values as in **R v R**, or due to advances in technology or medicine, as in **Quintavalle**. Such changes and developments may mean there are gaps left in the law. Professor Hart recognised that creativity was necessary where the existing rules did not cover the situation and Lord Denning said, 'We fill in the gaps'. This is what has occurred in these cases, the existing rules did not cover the situation so the judges filled the gap in the law.

"At times judges may need to be creative because Parliament has not been clear enough in drafting the statute or because it is old and the language obscure. An example is the **Offences against the Person Act 1861**. The courts have difficulty interpreting words such 'grievous' and 'maliciously' as they are not used in the same sense today. If the wording is unclear the judge cannot use the literal rule so may have to be somewhat creative. This can result in conflicting case law and injustice.

"Although there are times when judicial creativity may be necessary, as shown above, there are strong arguments against it. Two important ones are that judges are neither elected nor trained to make law and secondly a judge's decision applies retrospectively. Using two of the above examples, in **Donoghue v Stevenson** the manufacturer was negligent but until the case he would not have been liable under the law. In **R v R** the man got a criminal conviction for doing something that was not against the law at the time. These cases highlight the problem with judges making law. **Lord Diplock** said 'Parliament makes the laws, the judiciary interpret them' and I agree that although there are valid arguments both for and against creativity and opinions differ, in most cases it would be better if an elected Parliament made the law – or at least confirmed any creativity on the part of judges by amending the law. This happened after all four of the above cases, and although Parliament did not always very quickly this seems a fair compromise in law making."

Task 13 Examination practice

Your plan may be different as there are many ways to approach all the concepts of law questions. The following is a guide on which you can build. You would need to develop the points a little and expand on the examples as you did in the tasks. Reference to the relevant tasks is incorporated into the guide.

Here is the brief plan again.

> ***An explanation of the rules of precedent and statutory interpretation***
>
> ***A discussion of whether judges make law, with examples and reference to the above***
>
> ***An evaluation of the extent to which judges make law, with examples and reference to judicial and academic opinions***
>
> ***An evaluation of the extent to which judges should make law, with examples and reference to judicial and academic opinions***

An explanation of the rules of precedent

> Explain the rules which allow flexibility because you are asked to consider the extent to which judges can develop law (overruling, distinguishing)
>
> Explain the rules that limit discretion as these reduce the extent to which they can do so (*stare decisis*, court hierarchy)
>
> Use appropriate examples to illustrate
>
> See Tasks 2, 4 & 9 for the above

An explanation of statutory interpretation

> Again emphasise the rules which allow flexibility to show the extent to which judges can develop law (mischief rule, purposive approach).

Explain the restrictive approaches as these limit the extent to which they can do so (literal rule, golden rule)

Use appropriate examples to illustrate

See Tasks 3 & 4 for the above

Evaluate the extent to which judges make law

Critically analyse your discussion with reference to your examples and the opinion of others as to whether judges make law

See Task 8

Evaluate the extent to which judges should make law, with examples and reference to judicial and academic opinions

To evaluate you need to produce a balanced argument for and against judges making law, using and developing any examples from the earlier part of your essay

See Tasks 6, 7, 8 and 10 for material on the arguments for and against

See Task 11 for some judicial and academic opinions

See Task 12 for how to develop the cases or examples used

Write a concluding paragraph referring to the question asked – see below

Examination tip

The best way to remind the examiner that you have answered the actual question is to refer to it in your conclusion. What follows is a possible concluding paragraph, but it would need amending depending on your arguments in the main part of your essay.

"It has been shown that judges can develop the law to a large extent through precedent, especially by use of the Practice Statement in the Supreme Court. The extent to which they develop law is less when interpreting statutes, because even if judges use the purposive approach, they can refer to Hansard to discover, and therefore give effect to, the intentions of Parliament. I agree with Lord Denning and Professor Hart that judges should sometimes make law to 'fill in the gaps' where it is necessary to keep up with changing attitudes and technology. However, both academic and judicial opinions are divided on whether judges should make law and overall I feel it is better for an elected Parliament to do this."

This conclusion makes references to 'extent' and 'develop' and 'should' and tells the examiner the candidate is responding to the specific points raised by the question. Of course, this only works well if you *have* responded to those points in the main part of your essay.

The following abbreviations are commonly used. You may use them in an examination answer, but write them in full the first time, e.g., write 'actual bodily harm (ABH)' and then after that you can just write 'ABH'.

General

Draft Code – A Criminal Code for England and Wales (Law Commission No. 177), 1989

CCRC Criminal Cases Review Commission

ABH actual bodily harm

GBH grievous bodily harm

D defendant

C claimant

V Victim

CA Court of Appeal

HL House of Lords

SC Supreme Court

Acts

S – section (thus **s 1** Theft Act 1968 refers to section 1 of that Act)

S 1(2) means section 1 subsection 2 of an Act.

OAPA – Offences against the Person Act 1861

In cases – these don't need to be written in full

CC (at beginning) chief constable

CC (at end) county council

BC borough council

DC district council

LBC London borough council

AHA Area Health Authority

J Justice

LJ Lord Justice

LCJ Lord Chief Justice

LC Lord Chancellor

AG Attorney General

CPS Crown Prosecution Service

DPP Director of Public Prosecutions

AG Attorney General